When the Air Inhales You

MÁIGHRÉAD MEDBH

When the Air Inhales You

ARLEN
HOUSE

Published in 2009 by
ARLEN HOUSE
an imprint of Arlen Publications Ltd
PO Box 222
Galway
Phone/Fax: 353 86 8207617
Email: arlenhouse@gmail.com

Distributed in North America by
SYRACUSE UNIVERSITY PRESS
621 Skytop Road, Suite 110
Syracuse, NY 13244–5290
Phone: 315–443–5534/Fax: 315–443–5545
Email: supress@syr.edu

ISBN 978–1–903631–53–9, paperback
(a signed, numbered limited edition is also available)

Typesetting ¦ Arlen House
Printing ¦ Betaprint
Cover Images ¦ Seán Gilmartin, and the
Buckley family

CONTENTS

Acknowledgements to the editors and publishers of the following where poems were first published.

'Unified Field' is published in Jessie Lendennie (ed.), *Salmon: A Journey in Poetry 1981–2007* (Salmon Poetry, 2007). 'Hyperborea' was published in *Orbis*, 132, Spring 2005. 'Turning Point' won fourth prize in the Academi Cardiff Poetry Competition 2002. 'Madwoman in the Second-hand Shop' was published in John McNamee (ed.), *Out to Lunch* (Bank of Ireland Arts Centre, 2002). 'Offerings' was commissioned by the Irish Volunteer Association for use in greeting cards, October 2001.

Part 1

SATURN'S LITTLE COLOURS

Dedicated to Pat Griffin:
teacher, friend, enduring presence.

UNIFIED FIELD

For one moment when you express the source,
when the hard chatter of your tongue
turns to silver silk and slides you to the wind;
for a moment when the air inhales you
and you rest in its transparency like a
thought you don't know you're thinking –
wouldn't you live this jacketed life?

For one moment when saffron bursts from your belly
like a lesser sun and you know how it feels
to be a thousand spears of light;
for a space out of time, the ocean of all the tenses
beneath you with its nonchalant waves,
and you a cap on those waves, blowing off –
wouldn't you stick this sucking earth?

And when, in the last heave, you've gone to ground,
scattered, ash to dust, downed with ocean-bed bones –
isn't that the same as expressing the source,
supersonic silk, thought without thinking,
morning saffron, the absence of tense,
a cap taken by a breeze?

SATIN, MARIE

Don't go yet, Marie.
There might be something you've forgotten.
Just because you're at this level of the game,
where the spiked room is closing in,
doesn't mean you'll not move on.
You might yet reach the mountain top
where you look back,
survey what you've overcome
and go sliding down,
bonus points clocking up –
enter your name, you're a winner.

Take your hand.
Bring it on a tour of your body,
over those whitish hills and valleys,
buggying on the face of the moon.
You hate your difference from so many others –
models, academics, lawyers, doctors.
You've taken your directions from their maps,
but you're a foreign country.

Lose yourself. It's the only freedom.
In a land without names, you'll discover
your secret history.
You can rule, end the war.
Be at ease that whatever is scorched and desolate
can be reclaimed.

Lie down in satin, Marie,
because everyone deserves to rest.
The confused have a right to wake in beauty
and burn the lice-loved straw.
Etch your limbs in gold, silver, clay or sand.
You are a natural artist, god in your own cause.

*Saturn's Little Colours

In this cell, very little sings that isn't a whip.
There's a jailor in the corner beside the cold iron grate.
When he moves he breathes grey.
Petals blow in through the bars at the window.
The jailor catches them in his fist.
'Enjoy these', he says, 'but it will cost'.
You reach for the colour glowing between his knuckles,
searching your pocket with your other hand.
'I only have a few coins'.
He frowns.
'Pupil', he rasps, 'these petals are money.
Pledge me your bones and you can have them'.

* In Astrology, Saturn represents restriction, fate and the
hard, but fair, task-master.

PARTING SONG
In memory of Bridgie Kelly, Achill Island

Out here we all sing,
ravens, crows or linnets, wooden flutes or foghorns.
Shed skin, chestnut-smooth or orange-peel-puckered,
tight as a drum or saggy as an elephant,
all sends its tune, little ingénue, small starter
among the skies.

Listen to you now
on your deathbed, frail woman with the sweet voice.
'Prop me up, I want to sing my song'.
And you do. You're hardly more than eyes,
two shiny chestnuts in a leafless tree,
but your voice is as clear as the air out here.

Out here we all sing.
You know we do. We've been your backing.
When you sang 'Eileen MacMahon'
among the pans, dusted with flour,
the tide you felt was the rush of our voices
buoying you, your own personal sea.

Bridgie Kelly,
married young and widowed early,
always half-widowed, your husband a migrant worker;
you were sometimes in your voice,
sometimes in your tears,
sometimes in your hands, a brief rainbow.

Out here we all sing,
enemies and bosom pals. Faceless, we're not concerned
with placing or privilege.
You'll be side by side with Maria Callas, small diva,
big as a goddess despite your short path
from cottage to hill and back.

You could say we don't care
and that we care the best. All words with no tone.
But when the flesh starts to flag as it does now,
we're thrilled as midwives at every birth.
Here's the head, oh yes it's coming, and the first cry
is a melody, little novice, brave starter
upon our wings.

CAGED

It's simple: in all things go for liberation.

The laws still hold:
that the body contains us;
only birds have wings;
and we are not, like moles,
safe against the light.
But look at it this way:
cage bars are gapped;
the bones are inside the skin.
We are already part outside our prison.

Let go so of your grand obsessions,
your pacing of the ten by ten,
your close, repeated examinations
of every centimetre of ground.
This may not be the world.
If you put your finger through two bars
you'll feel the wind.
Listen and you might hear a whispered story.
To learn is no burden.

You were given a pack of cards yesterday.
It lies scattered in the corner,
displaying its sad and promising futures,
the 'If' axis waiting for a frame of flesh.
You found the King of Diamonds too brash,
the Queen of Hearts a wound weepy as a baby,
and the Knave of Spades swung his sword
in a way that made your stomach start.

There are always messages that confuse.
People chatter close by. When they're gone
you make your own gossip, helped by the honing flies
and the hunched musings of spiders.

Have you tried moving the cage?
A new position would at least alter the view.
A different path might bring new walkers,
people who wouldn't see the bars.
Don't you know that belief can cause visions?
Don't you know that fear causes visions?
When large thoughts knock, let them in.
Let them play their cards among the others.
One day the changing light might show you
a trump that bears your own face.
It will be right then, even easy,
to put it in your pocket and walk.

HYPERBOREA
for John S.

Mary Mooney sits bemused, her desk removing from
the line, the slant and twist of shoulders, and that shallow
clerks' chat. Soaps their tea-time topic. Poor subject for a
one-time queen, unseated in Atlantis by a quick
coup, the age of tyrants launched by her elder brother.
He, brutal with a scalpel, made of her a lab rat,
sailed her insides and extracted eggs. The hypnotist
told her what he'd said: 'Traitor to the cause of progress,
wanting families small and close, you hug like a child
tired old ways and stupid, slow, ox-encumbered methods.
You would never bring the island to its destined strength'.

Exploration I

> *In 1631, Luke Foxe,*
> *looking for the Straits of Anian,*
> *sailed north and saw Ne Ultra,*
> *Hudson Bay, at sixty-four degrees,*
> *'where the passage I hope doth lie'.*
> *Eighty-eight years on, James Knight,*
> *in search of the same north-west passage,*
> *'fifteen hundred miles cross from sea to sea',*
> *wintered at Marble Island.*

Her death was slow. That sullen gang, spawned of
comfort, weaned
on greed, had instruments of torture, types of pressing
so designed that bones would scream before they broke.
Her self-
control was very fine. She made Atlantis' beauty
shine before her eyes and praised it until breath had
drained
and pain shut down her nerves. Knives she used for
hunting made

shards of her body for the dogs. This explains her bouts
of panic, night's obsidian heavy on her chest,
her throat drying out, the heart a riot. And those pains
each lunar month, those blood tides, are tears for slaves
who knew
no flesh mother. This is her saving map, Cleito's heir.

Exploration II

> *Knight's crew disappeared.*
> *Later explorers, looking for traces,*
> *found only Inuit graves near the hut.*
> *The ships might have been damaged*
> *approaching the harbour at low tide.*
> *Winter, as always, had been harsh,*
> *and it seems that Knight should not have trusted Foxe,*
> *who said the cove was safe in all weathers.*

Henry has his own cartography, the earth a disk
flat as a pancake, the pole a rim that tips you off
to endless unmapped space. No satellite has probed that
ether, tv coverage or none. At NASA's base
he's watched those pencil clusters fume, magicians' wands to
bend the mind and conjure up illusions. Such trouble
leaders take to show us planet earth's a ball! Soccer,
no wonder, is the game of millions. Suckers, netting
native brain power in lies. Three hundred Flat-earthers
face the hard truth. Against the wall of the world's disdain
they hold tight to their convictions. Enlightenment hurts.

Exploration III

> *In 1725,*
> *Senex's map showed nothing in the Northwest territories.*
> *In 1778,*
> *Captain Cook, sailing by North America, wondered*
> *what could have induced Mr Staehlin*
> *to produce 'so erroneous a map,*

in which many of these islands
are jumbled in regular confusion
without the least regard to truth?'

You wizard Dame Street out of time by the power of
your eye. The Central Bank's a ziggurat and, druid,
you move in leaps. Another life they knew your worth. Now
you'll get no job fitting for your gifts. Like Captain Cook,
you're working with a faulty map. You stir up waves in
bourgeois pubs, you're with a queen. The gentler clubs leave your
name at the door. Your trappings, after all, are mostly
smiles. Sundays at sacred sites with Henry, Mary and
their likes, you track spirals and walk the hidden leylines.
You love their eyes, never damning, and their weaving hands.
Bruised hearts, searching for a kinder route, this New Age of
exploration.

Exploration details are from Glyn Williams, *Voyages of
Delusion* (HarperCollins, 2003).

Her face is close to mine.
I can see how she got here,
how she worked her way through the wood
with unrested sense,
hiding, then finding food.

Although her pack don't want her,
she'll survive.
She carries their rejection
in the deeper burrows of her fur,
letting it discolour her only a little.

She has walked alone for endless no-change days
and the pain is sometimes less.
You can see the rough sadness in her eyes
and the judgement in her naked teeth.
You can't lack this much and not seethe.

She has learned.
Being timid was never the way to gain respect.
When the desire takes her
she'll kill without thought,
then rest, fellowless, in the clearing.

Her fur is dirty yellow.
Nothing to be vain about.
She could fade but for two things –
her love of new prey
and her body's manic clinging to itself.

She knows she's a killer.
That leaves her free for kindness,
the odd time,
to a human or a bird.
She doesn't fret that she wasn't born generous.

WOLF WISDOM
for Aonghus

When the wolf comes nuzzling your knee,
don't say no.
Give him a smile, stroke the fur of his ears
and let him lead.

His road is varied and old as yours.
Sometimes it's easy,
then fraught with rogue branches, sudden drops
and enemy roars.

Be soldier to any climb,
but savour the downslope.
When the light's plenty gives you a rainbow,
it's sliding time.

Roam together by rivers that snake
through crystalline caves,
where waterfalls are trying to be rainstorms,
all rush and break.

At each day's end, lay your head down
on the wolf's purring belly.
You, like he, need only live,
both wise-born.

Innocence is always small, or so we perceive it,
a glowing pearl in the fearsome shell of the world.
Guilt is a dump full of life's scattered energies and
we could all end up there, unless we model our lessons
into something new. And sometimes it's not so hard.
You stop to rest and suddenly see a piercing shine in the murk.

You move towards the small thing, through the distraction
of voices, flailing vegetation and coaxing quicksand.
You find it's not only sweet, but a safe point from which
to view the flux. Its single clear note is singing:
'Those things you thought lost have been re-formed.
You've made me by accident, solely by desire'.

BIG BONG

in thunder comes the breath of outer space
a ringing bell but bellring never reached
the deadline for departure is no time
nowhere precisely on no day a stray
event a chance to be a finite some   ·
the noise makes nothing clear says nothing safe
and every hold is blown with eructation

the somehow always sucking in has stopped
full lung is pain and pain is endless sound
it gets so thick and hot no tube can last
we make the spew of no direction home
get slow we're here and home's a caravan
collision quake we knock spots off our face
that ride with us and make our spin a path

we look at where and how far we're away
we make relations see how big we bear
a round a wheeling make a pattern sing
the same old thing we like the same old thing
we always sang but never thought the tune
was measured and repeated fugue on fugue
our knowing is a no to knowing no

division between being and the void
we'd unite again all of us would mush
if daisies didn't push the soil apart
volcanoes didn't burst and storms distend
slim rains go shadow-battling grass go gold
sly flora grow on half an inch of crust
new babies berries honey and the hive

a thunder takes the insides and the eyes
become a way to eat a hut to hide
the smallest thing looks outside for itself
reflections of its manner and its mind
when enemies have died come eat their flesh
one bite and innocence dissolves to run
again as hunger and the jabbing spear

to represent the provenance of touch
the lurch the burst unbearable enjoy
slipsoar and maybe never feel again
make ecstasy a prime noetic thing
too large to hold too large to let it go
in spread a mappa mundi fold a ball
we venture into darkness and we draw

conclusions build a hall with massive rise
project our image make the image good
we've learned division we create again
a mirror of our feardom and our dream
live in beneath enormous roofs that splay
and vaunt and play the part of some sad reach
that thinks it touches glory with a bell

SPEEDY
for Aonghus

only boys of five are allowed in there
where the shiny treasures burn
and at every corner yet to turn
is a witch or a wizard
or a monkey or a bee or a brontosaurus
or v is for vicuna vole and viper
staring veering towards you
on the speedy speed racer
you shout
'to the rescue POWER RANGERS
want a fight?
I'm the best I can beat anybody
I'm Batman
DADADADADADADADADADADADADADADADA
BATMAN
my Daddy is bigger than yours
he is so
necklaces are for girls
I'm not a girl oh no'

Go on tell me
what the treasure is that makes your face so freshly
looking into every game and book and scene you want
explained with an answer whether true or false / what's
the difference real or headstuff / what's the world but
what you make it / will you make it

Go on tell me
how I missed you growing bigger / walking further /
racing from my side / joining sheets together / sailing
down the wall / building fences / running off on me like I
did to mine / until you turned round one day and asked
'what are you doing here?' / and I couldn't remember

Go on tell me
how I'm shocked that you repeat my ways and phrases
and most likely my defiance / how I forgot I'd be a parent
not another child to you / how I stand here while you do
revolutions around me / straining at the reins / bursting
to be free in a way I thought I'd be

Go on tell me
how at five years you're a person often bigger than a
crowd / how you know what I'm thinking / pick up all
that I feel / how your sympathies and cruelties are
soluble as sums / how I've lost my safe bets from the day
that you were born / how I love you like a hunger / fear
you like a storm

IF YOU WERE A CHILD WITH SEVEN EYES
for Fionn

If you were a child with seven eyes
I'd ask you to take a spoon,
then run like a hare to the end of the road
and get on a flight to the moon.

I'd ask you to go to the moon's dark side
for some dust as yellow as gold,
then rush back to earth, not spilling a drop,
and scatter it over the world.

If you were a child with seven eyes
I'd ask you to dig a hole,
put moondust in to cushion the fall,
then send all your troubles down.

If you were a child with seven eyes
you'd see how the magic was done:
seven colours sprung from the lunar cup
to wrap you up tight and warm.

If you were a child with seven eyes,
you'd walk as if earth were the sky,
with a spring in your toes and wings at your heels,
seven angels around you, a light on your head,
a pillar before you to guide you to bed,

and look, you have seven eyes.

GENERATION

Not these dollish cheeks, these still quiffs,
these babybird mouths, but the closed eyes
of dream contain them, our two sons.
Off they've flown to their secret places,
mine on the flattened back of his stuffed grizzly,
yours on the sweet wand of his thumb.
They explore caves under the cliffs,
take waterfall showers,
fight battles on high-speed aircraft,
pit themselves swarthy in wrestling rings.

They've left us their hollow sculptures,
pretty-as-pictures, child to the childness.
You could lose yourself in these works of art,
unlearning the roads to return to source.
Your fingers crab-crawl on my waist and stomach,
as we stand at their door, illicit partners.
In my own room, where you're still a visitor,
we remember how it began.
We do our own flying,
moulding our bodies the shape of joy,

tracing the contours of generation,
artists touching down.

LITTLE DARLING

Little Darling,
here's your plate of chips,
the pizza you ordered,
the remote control to keep your fingers supple
and the playstation to test your prowess
in the noble art of virtual combat.

Later we'll take you to the sports shop
where you can choose which brand you'd like this week –
Nike, Adidas or Reebok –
so you can outdo your friends
when you're all sitting in the front-room,
kick-boxing each other's alter-egos.

You're such an expert, Darling,
on all the Internet offers,
which clubs you can join,
what Java or Shockwave updates are available,
the latest kids' mailing lists.
Such a clever boy too with that new language,
txt mssgng.
Aren't you great to make do without vowels!

You know all the coolest adjectives and phrases,
and you're thrilled that we're all sounding like
Americans now,
because, really, that's where it's at,
isn't it, Darling?

THE GREENING OF MEMORY
Written at the request of artist Deirdre Carr to respond to some of her work

I want to be wrapped in your silky shoots,
your pea-green fingers, mother, pull me up.
I've been under your roots for too many years.
Can't you feel me suck? It's unnatural.
I dreamed I was driving, mother,
and I couldn't see the road.
The view in the mirror was such a hijack,
every time I looked I was looking back.
Your eyes were tongues in a leaf-green mouth
and I had to hold on so you could sing me,
sing me, in one long, open note.

You once were the sun in a faceless field,
the sea-horse smile I sailed,
the duckdown pillow, the crisply sheet,
clean and never stealing.
But you took yourself to some height,
left me cold and nameless.
What would I be? The apron, the laugh,
the ear, the wit, the charleston steps?
You had become a white mountain
and I had to bring safety gear –
pillow and pick – in case you knocked me down.

I wanted to live in your voiceless white,
so high I was invisible. I called you to help me up.
'On the summit I'll see the world, won't I,
and an eagle will land on my shoulder?'
I saw footprints behind me.
A snow-trick maybe. I was aching,
stacking step upon step in that chill,
until I was lying on the summit with a cloudy view.

Shocked then by a vision of myself,
pale, hunched and crusted,
a long cut above the dimple of my neck.

At last came another vision: you and I,
stitching together in a large bay window,
like two women of your generation,
speaking our pasts in colours.
Duty is a whispering room,
where names are held in the timbre,
never in the captured word.
I asked you: 'Will red cuts on white mountains
ever be heard so well the snow melts
and bloodfed roots turn to green?'

You didn't answer straight.
Instead, like a great bird,
you took your smile and screeched through the house,
seven times through and around,
back to guide my hands.
I stitched a name I'd never heard,
red bleeding into green, too long
to read. I was lost in the letters, swept
back to the white summit, a red hole in my head.
Our bodies were the mountain, our heads the mountain.
I stood and you shattered to acres of green.

I could choke, mother, on your silky shoots,
and your sap that rises like flame.
You're the wind in my blood
and the sun at my back,
and I'd die at the tips of your pea-green fingers,
but you're pushing up, up, up.

TURNING POINT

That was the year his father grew into his bones;
up through the marrow like a liquid tree
that hardened and stretched the mould.
The living past died in his spinal core,
stiffened his joints, made an angle at his waist
and flattened his feet as if they were hobnailed zones.

His skin renewed itself, slower, but much as before.
Only Bronagh noticed how his forehead tightened
when another bill got floored.
Stiff in the morning, shuffling in slippered feet,
the smallest issue, a spillage of milk,
broke the back of his mustered will to cope.

It was the year of strikes and foot-and-mouth disease,
when funeral pyres turned the air slate
and farms became silenced compounds.
Nothing ran. Buses and trains stood mute.
Cars and trucks lurked at the border,
cornered like insects by the spray's sterile advance.

Dotcom companies failed, thousands owed;
every day more lettings go.
The floods came and swallowed the fields,
chewed the bank of the river and spat it out.
The path ended at a new place
and winter brought the longest snow for years.

She saw the sense in all the manic sweeping
and so did he, a natural wisdom
where deep-rooted things survive
and everything unstable ends its time.
Still, when his own dream burned,
his father's effigy grinned in the fire's eye.

The failed farm of his childhood, his parent's retreat
into the dark corners of the house, the split,
glitched his ecliptic, and he stood at the door,
rubbing his forehead. Bronagh had begun to leave.
Not age but history was turning him old,
the cruel wheel brandishing its spoke.

I press my palm against your back in passing –
I'm feeling generous today –
and my fingers almost touch the nape of your neck.
You used to like it when I stroked you there,
a long time ago, before the air between us froze
and left us trapped like forgotten mountaineers,
our eyes open but expressionless,
our hands in a parody of reach
across the great translucent divide.

I can't remember when we stopped the struggle
and let the colour fade to glaze,
but I recall a moment when my cheeks were wet
and I didn't know this victim heart,
or this body with no hope, for the one that heaved and rippled
at the breezes that your hands could conjure up.
There was too much pain. I left it.
All desire is frozen now,
veins within this misty box, pre-history.

My skin has loosened from the bone. Don't touch it.
All the mirror shows is time.
Still, my hand upon your covered shoulder and our bodies close,
the double bed we've never cut in half,
are comforts we can offer, without rancour, free.
I'm sure we're a story in the silent sky,
some stellar logic to it all,
my fingers roots that train us to the soil,
indulgent amber framing us in place.

It wasn't that intemperate lashings of wind drew grids on his face,
or that his youth was spent driving against a hoarding sea
for the prize of an edible fish.
It wasn't that he lived by the side of Etna
or sea-legged it on an unstable piece of ground.
No wild movements of nature made him rabid,
but aren't we great impersonators?

The clustered dwellings of cities
are overcrowded trees,
full of racketing and bickering.
We kick the flightless to their deaths,
jostle for breeding places.
You might say we offer a hand to the weak,
but no-one rises without desire.

He was one of the fallen, who, by dint of will,
rocketed himself into the race
and still sparked when the contest was done.
I wonder if there's any other meaning
to this fight for life than the fight itself,
how everything sings its own raw song,
does its own dance, however frantic or flailing,
lost in the rantings of a private tornado belt.

Her husband-hunk is out in the Irish sea,
two weeks on and two weeks off an oil rig.
He turns black out there, comes home like a model,
a siren sheen on his midnight skin.
White piano keys his teeth are then.
She plays them like a maestro,
only with her tongue, a moonlight song.

She's tried the undie in the pocket trick.
It could be anyone's, no matter what he says.
Letting on her Dunnes Stores lace was Michelle Pfeiffer's,
he could be moving to the wrong tune. Lethal.
It's only seagulls he could have,
but she's still measled green.
The wind that shimmies on his arm, the sheet on top,

the working clothes that cling to his body, damp,
the tools that snuggle panting in his hands –
she wants them all ravened by the black tide,
and only him and her on the platform above the swell,
Noah and wife all over again.
'A blue background?' asks Hugo Finn, photographer.
'Oh yes', she says, 'and soft focus, dreamlike'.

'The blue brings out the colour of your eyes.
Relax', he says. She leans her shoulders back
on the studio's kitten-soft *chaise longue*
and wonders if that's what he meant. Her cheeks turn rose.
'That's good', he says. 'Now don't be shy.
Picture it's Valentine's Day and
he's come home with flowers for his love'.

'Do you think I'm silly?' 'No', he says,
'I think that Peter Burke's a lucky man'.

She's glowing now, vermilion inside,
her eyes ripe swollen grapes, her breasts aglaze with sweat.
'Perhaps a little risqué touch,
one hand under the head,
the other on your hip. Look, like this'.

He drapes her fingers over her curve like lace,
a white glove against the black. Her skin quivers.
She's a sculpture fit for a boulevard, is what
his hands are saying. He's smoothing back her hair,
brushing bright on her biceps as he goes.
He straightens her shoulder strap and blows away

a wispy strand. They laugh. Then back behind
the lens he's making goddesses of her,
the loving ones. Frame by frame she dawns
a little more, her mythic tale exposed and printed
in her eyes, impressed upon her skin
as sure, as resolute
as the three by three her husband-hunk will hold.

MORALITY MAN

You mistake desperation for passion.
Your outbursts are fraught
with that quest you're on
for the right line on everything.
Morality man, the Gavel made flesh.

Bolts should shoot from my fingers
and knock you up against the wall, bewildered.
Coward. I save it for the innocent,
the little child who sits nut-eyed and amazed,
then leaks fruity tears into this tragic scene
of his mother banging doors,
yelling so you'll hear, clattering saucepans,
while you, desperate or passionate,
seem to sleep.

INHERITANCE

Jim's father knows the names of trees
and killed pigs in his time
down in the arsehole of nowhere.
No black tie affairs for him,
nor sitting at the top table with the minister.
He never met a millionaire
nor shook hands with acclaimed gurus
of world economic highways.
He was never asked for his opinion
on CNN or national television,
never even answered a market survey.

At night he watches TV,
Sundays takes the collection at the parish church,
his only stand as a pillar of the community.
He worries about his leg, the rising price of food
and the scuts who would travel all the way
from Dublin to rob a pensioner.
He keeps a shotgun for them, sweets for his
grandchildren.

Jim has begun to stand flat on the ground,
tilted forward at the waist like a wooden bird.
He places his scooped hands on his hips
and surveys the acclaim he musters,
valuing it at little more than effort
if his children weren't there.
He closes his eyes when he's embarassed,
rubs his hand across them as his father does,
and smirks when relating events
he's almost too shy to share.

They talk rarely,
which is probably why they don't know
that they're both suckers for a child,
fuss over details, dinners and unwashed hands,
that each has a white-hot temper,
that they are graceful and graceless
in the same strained way, almost carbon-copied,
except that one has carried the hod
further out into the world.

LIONHEART
In memory of William Buckley

1

You have done your time.
I no longer need the moral epithets,
that arsenal of fear,
between me and your harm.
Look, I'm taking the lock from your cage,
where you have never tired of your efforts to thrive
or pit yourself against the bars.
Raise your head.
You're free to travel my eyes,
ride the inner lines, buzz on my signal avenues.
Come in.
There's a place of comfort for everyone,
and you, with your lion's nature, need repose.

II

Once a soldier, always battling,
fighting too for beauty
among the reticent stars
and the nobler novelists –
Dickens, Dostoevsky, Chekov.
Your stomach fed upon itself as cruelly
as the woman in the woods on children.
You ran from it, but when you turned a corner
your heart rattled, pounced,
did tarantellas that were no cure.
The enemies surrounded you again.

Besieged, you did all you knew
to build a habitable fort.
Your prophylactic foodstuffs were inspired
in a generation that believed the faster lie.
These were your middle names:

honey, garlic, mint, onion, beetroot, nettle,
carrageen, seaweed, lemons, bananas, olive oil,
brown bread and chew-your-food-a-hundred-times.

You were my first audience
as I strutted and jumped,
displaying my Bunty-schooled ballet steps.
You would mouth the dance tunes,
from Tchaikovsky to a diedle.
You were my art critic,
let me spread twenty cloned, paper faces
like patches on your bedspread
and pronounced no hard judgement.

You never forgot to bring me sweets.
I was the one you would love,
your right-hand child,
the fruit that proved your life creative.
You took me everywhere.
We were a strained and silent pair,
and, like most adults,
you must have thought your child
a tougher thing than you.

You believed us close,
bought me one Christmas a bracelet and chain,
another, Chanel No. 5,
the only perfume you knew.
I had nowhere to go.
Every man, as the tired tale recants ...

A friend who read the cards
saw a strong man with a big heart for me.
I thought you had none.
You had terrorised family and street.
What I remembered were
the loner's hands choking my waist
and a mind with no gift for rapport.

I have tried to measure the worth of different loves,
listened to the chattering of cliques
who think of people as flags they wave or burn.
From friendless to friendless a hand is stretched
in terror and distrust.
Every man, yes, and every friend.

III

You have done your time.
How much did you deserve?
I have often thought myself the angel
of protection and revenge.
Let that go.

Come in.
The room is full of flowers.
I'm placing a cushion at my back
and a footstool at my feet.
I'm drinking your health with a fine red wine.
You have taught me the ways of the lion,
to carry my nature with purpose,
to cry alone.

You raise your head
and I greet an ill-fitting man,
who needs, like all creatures,
a stamp that says he's approved, bona fide.
Love is an opening of the hand
and I will no longer deny the quality you yearned for,
your periodic sunbursts of joy,
your times of generous giving,
your time for a child.
And that you loved me as well as you ever could.

OUT OF MY SKIN
Rap. Of a woman in Inner City Dublin

Too many people moved in.
One son, three sons and him.
My body was a blistered tin,
the light always on, my bed in the kitchen,
questionings, chatter and din.

I packed and moved out of my skin,
took a hatchet, a hammer and pins,
made a rickety tent to live in,
patched up with rags, pegs always shifting,
hail and high water for kin.

When the rain would come up to my chin,
I'd crawl back under my skin,
with one son, three sons and him.
I'd make it all neat as a pin,
shear the sharp ends, shine up the mirrors,
drown conversation with gin.

It was never too long till again
I'd take hatchet, hammer and pins,
hack a branch for the roof of my tent,
pin a patch on and batter pegs in.
No-one came calling. For fixing and selling
they went to the house of my skin.

In the end I grew scales and a fin,
took up hatchet, hammer and pins,
slid the hatch from a pore and swam in.
They had fought and kicked over a bin,
scattered the plastic, spattered the milk,
cut their flesh on a broken tin.

I picked up the overturned bin
and swept all the furniture in.
I washed from the floor to the ceiling,
including my three sons and him.
I pointed the way, I guided them down,
past the knee-cap and out of my skin.

THE RIVER WARD STEALS MY EYES
The River Ward flows through Swords, Co. Dublin

I cast my eyes in the river and the river flowed on.
It flowed straight, it flowed askew.
It flowed past the daisies and the broken ash,
past the leafless tree, past willows,
past the boys with the cans
and the girls with the fags,
past the old men and the dogs,
past the women on their unislim walks,
past rabbit burrows and badgers' noses,
past the furze and its golden purses,
past the sinewy lane that never at midnight,
past wolf whistles and giggles,
past the curses, the sweet papers, past the bonfires,
past the cider bottles and the bad plans,
under the wooden bridge, under the stone bridge,
through Mondays, through Friday nights.

I cast my eyes in the river and the river flowed on.
It flowed straight, it flowed askew.
It flowed past the castle and the ancient church,
past the rowan tree, past hazel,
past the houses on the crest
and the council estates,
past the tall men and the squat,
past stone of centuries and baby oak,
past dog-rose and dripping fuchsia,
past the mango fox by starlight,
past abandoned trolleys and burnt-out cars,
past costume rings and bracelets,
past the whitethorn and blackthorn, past the fairy hill,
past the spooning couples and the hot hands,
over the bike wheel, around the rusting car,
through sunsets, through winter snow.

I cast my eyes in the river and the river flowed on.
It flowed straight, it flowed askew.
It flowed past the schoolbags and the whirring bikes,
past shoe-black berries, past lawns,
past the soggy grass and the caterpillars,
past the loners and the lost,
past those who fish and those who throw,
past quickened footsteps and the drawn knife,
past the one heron at mid-day,
past fiery thrushes and their morning rows,
past pipers and pigeons the trees try to echo,
past joggers and loungers,
past the mitchers, the militants, past the winos,
past the screaming housewife and the dreaming child,
under the long kiss, under the sharp slap,
through property slumps, through high tides.

I cast my eyes in the river and the river flowed on.
It flowed straight, it flowed askew.
It flowed past the runners and the crossed knees,
past blown leaves, past petals,
past the meeting of friends
and the nights we forgot,
past the dour days and the rich,
past the picnic and the library book,
past final exams and parents' hackles,
past tomorrows and planned conversations,
past blood and slow dances, past sudden goodbyes,
past tall thistles and brambles,
past the swallows and blue tits, past the jackdaws,
past the bite the flood made and the new path,
over the dead man, under the low cloud,
through funerals, with summer bands.

I cast my eyes in the river,
bubbles in the river,
cast my eyes in the river
and the river flowed on.

It might be because the moon is full in Pisces
that the woman in the St Vincent de Paul shop
is telling her story to the clothes on the rail.
The grannies behind the counter smile.
One of them whispers, 'She's just out of hospital'.
Not cured, it seems, of her many grievances.
'What kind of a world is it if you can't speak your mind?
All I said was I didn't like it. She rolled up her newspaper
and bashed me over the head. They kicked me out then.
What was I supposed to do? I didn't want to draw blood.
There he was with the shillelagh, ready to beat me with it
and I troubling no-one. It's a disgrace, that's what it is'.

She has a rapt audience. Only the odd, discreet rustle.
Evening dresses get a high spotlight
as she fingers them and makes them twirl.
The lace collar of a blouse brings on a new outburst
and she's lost to her own script, as big on stage as any great,
as central to her moment as Fionnuala Flanagan or Olwen Fouère.
The women let her be. They've seen worse.
For all her talk, she finds a coat she wants to buy,
a woollen salt and pepper that will keep her company
as she battles the windy streets of Swords this winter,
proclaiming to the paving stones and the iron benches
the cruelty of the race, life's high treason, her innocence

and other madnesses.

THE BEATING

It was a stretched and vacant day, boiled as a bullseye.
Under the sky's big top all that was missing were clowns,
a high trapeze, two elephants, three Pomeranian dogs,
a lion, two tigers, a family of gymnasts from Czechoslovokia,
who also did the Tonto act, a ringmaster's whip.

Mistress of the centre-ring, I queened it over buttercups
    and bluebells.
I turned conductor to the grape-green grass and made it play
a fanfare as I skirted the scorching tar, directed
footsteps, knees high, back straight, toes diving down.
Small birds dusted the trees and gave their eyes

to my brave struts, my fine preening, my tail-coat swagger.
Once in an hour a car would pass and I would suddenly
sit, take a blade of grass and shred it, pensive as a cat
with a dead catch. For five minutes I forgot my public and parade
and found myself at our neighbours' gate, staring at their curtains.

Missus wore her hair streaming, like a princess
thrown from the castle, left wandering forever without comb or
pillow to lay it under. She told us she had been beautiful,
had kept her trousseau in a lined drawer in her father's careful
house, but had married a serpent in disguise.

Earlier, she had sat in our house and darned my brother's
sock, my mother's ruse to make her worried woman's
hands feel useful. She said he'd finish her off when he came home.
Beating the badness out of her, that's what he said he was doing.
An amateur exorcist, undermining men in black.

How do they train the circus animals? Pretty pomme dog
becomes puppet, the elephant a pet, the tiger a calm opponent.
Whack! I'm a reliable witness. An implement was used.
The leg of a chair I believe she said. And a scream and a whack.
The curtains swayed as if they wanted to start a show.

The circus ended. Still dazed, a sullen girl with tangled hair,
walking the ground where the caravans stood, searched for a
boy with black eyes and gravelled skin. A crumpled
and discarded ticket became the souvenir she stuffed
like an insole in her ring-master's boots before she turned away.

When my hand meets yours, we might end up confused,
in the touching forget who moved first, whose need
brought us to this side-by-side seat, this roused
state where the air has begun to scatter seed.
I came to teach you reading. You taught me what
you knew of birds nesting in the hills, where
you escaped from a vicious school and a hot-
headed father. You found gems in the hushed lairs.
We drop pennies into the well of answers,
knowing all our actions give thanks or deny.
We might be the butterfly clapper that stirs
our own healing wind, a balm we'd never buy.
Adam and Creator perform their dance in the round,
each by times in the cloud, by times on the ground.

THE VOLUNTEER
for Martin Buckley

'My life', he says, 'is broader than red.
It's brighter than a flag flown on a common mast.
It has electric blue in it and colours I can only feel.
It has breadth, height, depth, time and still other dimensions.
Before I was born, my mother spent months on her back
praying to a Saint who had given his coat to a beggar.
It was her generosity or his that fuelled my blood. Maybe both.
My work keeps me stretched, brings out the Mars in me.
I have friends, I play sport, and where others seek visions,
I give some hours each week to listen to people with whom
I can travel along a common path. If they paid me for that,
it wouldn't come near to being the force that brought
me live to the earth. It would be done for something other
than the painting of my life with off-spectrum colours
and the domino push of a gift passed on'.

We wear the colours of heat although this is a cold place.
We have escaped death to enter a grey waiting room,
where nothing we see reminds us of ourselves.
We sit with darkly-clothed people
who have dirt in the lines of their faces.
We have no such lines yet and our faces shine,
are more likely to ooze than dry out like theirs.

We are given homes on streets where litter
sails through the air like sand on a desert wind,
where concrete cliffs hide square caves
and their interior lives.
It's supposed to be safe here,
but we often feel it a kind of punishment.
Perhaps there's always a punishment for desiring too much.

Our neighbours hate us and hiss at us,
as if we were a hostile species.
And still, in some ways we are alike.
We all parade in bright colours,
although theirs are the colours of electricity
and ours those of animals and plants.
The girls cling like we do, keep each others' secrets.

Like us, they fuss over their lives,
as if they feared being taken from them.
They sing without a catch in their throats,
they spark when you meet their eyes.
In time we may become used to their fear
and they to ours.

Radio

You can touch me better in the dark,
where pores expand like pupils
and your words are fingers in a bowling ball,
rolling me on to crash
or dream moodily in the groove.

In the muffed backroom of the ear
all the lampshades are veiled
with red and gold chiffon squares.
I'm Lady Godiva in a town
of loyal curtained cottages.

In here, we're brought close.
We open our stories
and share them without fear.
You come in different shapes,
a song on a spring morning,

a call across a closeted estate.
When I was a child you were a pair of heels
clicking beneath an upstairs window,
while a man clutched his blanket
and wished himself dead.

I hear those footsteps still,
because they came from the dark
and sound seeps from like to like,
a mole drilling down.
Now I'm older, you're Pat Kenny,

Marion Finucane and callers,
who reach me in a quiet workroom
or console me in a traffic jam,
where I wish for another vehicle,
a private mystery train.

SCHOLAR
for James Buckley

We learn the forms of the world
in the crucibles of fear and love,
and we remember both in the end.
It's the learning we might try to forget –
how we sweated in a contracting cell,
while some pedant paced outside,
itching to award us worth or warp
in the corridors of space-time.

I remember conversations best,
when questions are piled on the table
like presents, opened with glee
and examined for themselves, warmly,
each one worth at least as much as its gesture.
Whenever illumination comes,
it travels best through open doors.
So save your teeth for that ready smile

that reflects the clarity of fire,
letting dialogue begin with a mirror
and end, who knows, with enlightenment or bathos,
in mind or foot, or go nowhere at all.
'At least', says the scholar, 'take a look at the thoughts
that have tiled the certainties of the past.
We have come into a fractured generation,
but we hope the breaks are those of an egg,

not of the earth's crust. There's no mother left
can cushion us with unfailing truths,
but we'll be forced into no small cell. We'll choose'.

We have been stalked by fear since the first night.
Tyrants and hunger have always linked arms.
We don't know how long we'll live to think,
and now the planet is as small as our uncertain fist.
But those who study can smile,

because there's a sense in which they are never old or young,
but forever at their desks with vellum and quill,
letting the light erupt from their fingers in a dialogue
of abandon and control.
For the scribes it was all care and precision,
and what has changed?
The glow of gold always draws an eye.
Don't they know, who have ever worked at a paper

or studied a book, that there's space to be found,
even in the smallest cell, and how many
would wait there, cold or not, for that one drop
of real insight that falls from the universal eye?
In there, porthole to the undarkened sun,
there are movements and explosions,
a way to value that is above pedant
and above president and above priest.

Those who study can smile,
because in the end they know
there is no end,
only ever the opening of one more porthole,
one more book,
and the lighting of one more candle
in an ever-expanding cell.

THE END OF THE WORLD
September 2001

In Tunisia they call it the end of the world,
where the salt lake meets the sky –
one pale canvas as large as the eye can take.
I have a place the same.
I've wandered far out on its pockered surface,
when the sky was lit by the sun's outriders,
and waited for the real presence.

The sun always keeps her appointments.
She's such a prima donna – a lighted stage,
an audience stanched of breath.
She has prepared herself with professional care,
preening in the green room behind the earth,
and here she steps up.
Soon you won't see her at all,
only her costume and the dazzle of her gifts,
but for ten minutes you can stare at her body
and not go blind.

We're always in the process of dying.
There are times I've misjudged the hour
and stood in the Chott like a misshapen outcrop,
a feeble standing stone set by a bad astronomer.
I have stood long enough for the fragile
skin beneath to get tired and groan.
Below is an abyss
that once digested fifteen hundred
camels and their drivers,
then closed back up, innocent-faced.

I'm never lost, just standing in the Chott
or falling. I always know I'm nowhere.

That might be better than the opposite,
than believing my tall towers
will stand to me when the ground belches.
It's older than Ozymandias,
this story of crust and crack.

I am afraid though. Of the same old story.
Of whatever shakes beneath the feet,
of poison in the air, of venom in the spittle of a tap.
If only everyone were the same,
and the earth a place where all children played
on beaches and kept the factories going
in buckets and spades and DVDs for rainy days.

Someone out there doesn't love me,
but is that the beginning or the end,
if the universe itself started with a split?
The beginning might have felt like the Chott giving way
and if you plumbed the dark,
maybe you rose an outrider of the great queen,
a particle of light in the sea-sky.

I'm playing my Tunisian CD, pop and malouf in cahoots.
If it comes to sides I'll not be the blue tent
that must mother its children through some hot god's grid,
but we're on the great salt canvas, where the enemy
could be your own weight, any hustle of scorched air,
or the hands you thought were friends.

A voice calls out that's it time to crouch down.
Maybe he sees himself in a blue tent.
I'm not doing that. I'm walking out into the blank
with two cans of paint and my fingers for brushes,
and like every artist before me,
I'll try to draw from featureless pale
a pattern that's old and new, pop and malouf,
put perspective on the flat.

Who knows when my hands' pressure
will cause the surface to collapse?
I'll fall then, like the camels, like the sun,
into the black and back.

Chott: *the name given to dry salt lakes in the Saharan region of Africa.*
Malouf: *a kind of music played in Tunisia which has its roots in Spain
and Portugal.*

CATWOMAN
aka Fashion Magazine Editor

It's your own scent you follow now,
back to where your other suit lies
limp and longing on its hook.
You're always doing this, alone
in the drip-damp night,
the day's champing tiger on hold.

A key's turn and the chasing rain
is sucked from its batter on your hair,
sent to find lesser prey.
You can't contain yourself. You shed
your outdoor coat,
your blinding shoes, those necessary skins.

Now you find it interesting
to let your finger brood, and not
your mind, upon a type of sleep.
It's barely touch, as you draw a line
from forehead to thigh,
sheathed in black, a lazy cat.

Today you hired a new designer,
signed two advertising deals,
heard your colours praised for style.
They said those orange tones, that tiger
thing was wild.
Your mouth warms to a monochrome smile.

Blast you from a height, you've taken up with someone else.
A French woman no less – more leg, more swagger, more
interesting bread.
She's got long hair, I'm sure, brown eyes, a permanent tan,
and smiles the sweet feminine smile I never had.

I left your bed. I said it first, the 'I-don't-love-you-anymore'.
You should have died, or at least crawled about the floor,
disabled by your loss, unable to perform your daily functions,
turned to unplanetary plasma by the pain of your forever love.

Not only should I keep the right to have and unhold,
I should see you squirm for all the days I spent in pain, bowing
to your insistent needs, living the way you approved, the quicksand
of my fear sucking my feet to your silent underground.

Blast you, now my heart is sore, as though you were swinging on it.
The door is long in closing. What I want and what I don't
are in a set dance, doing underarm twirls and linked rotations.
Behind is dark. Ahead is a small glow. I tell myself to breathe deep

and remember you're a new person whenever you go.

DESIRE

We are two beating
hearts on a bed, hoping to
beat each other red.

OPPOSITES ATTRACT

Jude the rude married
a prude. She was the wall. He
was the bouncing ball.

THE FIRST STEP

The small child is learning to walk.
His mother throws her arms out, inviting.
If the child can manage to run into her arms,
he will have proved his ability to stand alone.

LAST

It won't last, because nothing …
How do you know how long exactly this is taking?
Is it
     mean
     sidereal
     tropical
     standard
     summer
     solar
     lunar
     gross menstrual time?

How many days was it on Jupiter
whose great red spot
your red hot love
has stormed for three hundred our years at least?

Two hundred and sixty-four thousand four hundred and sixty
Jupiterian days of nine hours and fifty-five minutes
the spot has been visible.
That's one hundred and nine thousand five hundred and
seventy-five earth days of twenty three hours fifty six
minutes four point zero seconds mean solar time
but I rounded a figure off so that's not exact.

Venus takes two hundred and forty three earth days
to rotate on its axis –
          oh what a night!
The universe is thirteen billion years in the making;
think of all that
        attrition and
        contrition.

Because planets rotate
is that why we make this question
our poor doll pivot
and that tune our only comfort:
                        ah but will it last?

THE HEART'S DESIRE

'I'll give you all your heart desires',
said the mother to the child.
'Where's my heart?' asked the child.
The mother showed her.
For a long time the child sat,
feeling the beat of her heart,
then fell asleep.

'I'll give you all your heart desires',
said the mother to the child.
'I know my heart', the child replied.
'It's a steam engine going round,
like the planets, like the world'.
'But your heart doesn't move, my pet'.
'Yes it does, Mammy. Watch'.
The child ran round and round,
then took her mother's hand
and said, 'Feel my heart'.
The mother placed her hand against
the child's warm chest and thought,
This child has a long way to go.
Her heart is a bouncing ball.

'I'll give you all your heart desires',
said the mother to the child.
'What's 'desires'?' asked the child.
'Desire is gravity, my pet.
It's being drawn to something,
like a salmon to the river's source,
or a swallow to the heat'.
'Or a moth to a light bulb?'
'Yes, my dear. I'd turn the darkness
into light for you'.

'I'll give you all your heart desires',
said the mother to the child.
'I understand and thank you, Mammy',
the happy child replied.
'So what is it that draws you,
like a salmon, like a swallow?
Like a moth to a light bulb?
What calls your heart to follow?'
The child stopped and listened,
with a hand on her heart,
and closed her eyes.
Her mother sat, poised to provide.

'My heart is happy', said the child,
'to be a steam engine in my chest,
to pump itself from start to start
and roundabout, and sing its tune,
and, Mammy, you've given my heart its due,
because all my heart desires is itself'.

How to Make a Magic Carpet
with thanks to Gustav Davidson's A Dictionary of Angels

When the sun is in Capricorn and that perennial goat
is butting its shadow among the starched branches
on the dried-up skin of the soil; at the hour of the sun,
on a Monday, when the moon is full, let a virgin girl
weave a carpet of white new wool on a loom in her house.

Take the carpet on a Monday to where no human lives,
but brown rabbits, lightning foxes and shy badgers.
Lay it on the grass, lining east with west and, with a rattle
made of bones, describe a circle around it, so envious
spirits who poke with their fingers will be singed and cowed.

Raise your wand and call upon the angels of the bearings.
Draw them in: Michael from the East; Raphael North;
Gabriel, messenger of the west;
Miniel from the south, bringing love's breath to the ears.
Turn east and summon Agla, demon-fighter, god-named.

Before the wind turns, gather the points of the carpet around you
and chant, 'Agla Agla, Lord Almighty, force of nature,
spirit of the stars, ruler of the four divisions and their unity,
by the power of Thy Name, of the Tetragrammaton,
bless this covering in which I hope to fly'.

It has been said that God will hide the seeker under Their wings,
that we can trust to the cabin beneath Their feathers,
that through Their grace everything is held or falls.
Fold the carpet and now say:
'Recabustira, Cabustira, Bustira, Tira, Ra, A'.

You may use your carpet only when the time comes.
You'll know it for sure when your head threatens to detonate,
filled with metal pins, broken glass, nails and slate shards.

Hold out until a new or full moon, then creep to the quiet place
of hiding rabbits and badgers, bringing a parchment of azure blue,
Raziel written on it with the feather of a dove.

Light a fire, throw on a fist of incense, lie prostrate on your rug,
parchment in your right hand, wand in your left and call out:
'Vegale, Hamicata, Umsa, Terata, Yeh, Dah, Ma, Baxasoxa,
Un Horah, Himesere, Raziel, Tzaphniel, Matmoniel, Io'.
Then let them lift you, head unwound, flesh a forgotten weight,

into the white, unstraining hammock of the air.

Part 2

EITILT : FLIGHT

Dedicated to Máire Buckley:
sister, teacher, friend, the essential link.
Died 7 May 2006.

EITILT
Funeral address

Dearest Sister,
whose healing hands made cushions,
    made jumpers,
    made food,
    made better –

whose smile brought glamour to the grubbiest streets,
who flitted, Mercurial, from earth to air
with the ease of a heartbeat, the grace of a bird,
for whom the smallest gesture was the greatest gift,
and each gift that was given, pure gold –

who loved birthdays and Sundays and nights full of dance,
who worked like a Trojan and played like a child,
to whom every new moment was crystalline light
in which everything danced with its own bright feet
and the last thing on earth was a frown –

who was icing and tinsel, haute cuisine, good wine,
prized for her intellect, crowned for her looks;
firsts in debating, in English, in Maths,
as happy at study as making a cake,
whose cakes were creations of mind –

who never forgot the day you were born,
or that you were unique in your time,
who saw everyone's colour and everyone's sound
as the touch of an artist, the note of a song,
a part of a jigsaw, a gem –

who knew all we can see is only a speck
on an infinite canvas, and joining the dots
is the work of a million lifetimes in thought;
who was tireless and boundless and never afraid,
and followed her truth like a knight –

Sister –

let all of your thinking and all of your love
and all of your effort roll out,
make a carpet to fly on, a map of the world,
with colours from deep red to white.
Take a step on that runway, let space be your ground;
it's time to do just what you planned –
move into the light with your angels, your guides.
My heart has been wrenched and my skin has turned cold,
but I wish you your vision, your freedom to fly;
so saving your memory and holding your gifts,
the only redemption can be to consent
and say,
Dearest Sister,
Goodbye.

THE NEWS

The phone has grown huge and heavy in my hand –
herald outcrop of a new reality,
where nothing is close, not even the air.
Here the acid light that sends the vision strange.
Here the featureless stretch of a dry salt lake.
Here nothing grows, except bad news.

IN THE MORGUE

Life floodlit your face
with its untimed tides.
Your eyes glistened like jumping fish.

They've spelt your name wrong.
Maybe it isn't you.
There's not a feature I recognize.

My hand pauses above your face
and I peer, trying to find one familiar patch of skin.
You're a marble statue someone didn't like.

Through a fall of tears I touch your hair.
My hand swims in its silk
and I stroke it goodbye.

But the event that was you has gone already,
a stream eaten by a karstic landscape,
leaving nothing for the pilgrim but stone.

COPING

Since you've left, there are friends at every turn.
I'm talking, not being precious about my grief.
They say that's healthy.
My stomach churns and I wonder
if too much coping will erase you altogether.

Mirror Mirror

The mirror reveals me to the skull.
When you reflected, you were never so cruel.
Where shall I look for the necessary lies?

APPROVER

You had become the approver,
the one I carried in my head
to persuade myself I had a friend.

Your thoughts echoed mine,
ever the supporting opinion.
It seems my realities must stand alone or fall.

MODEST

Now that you're not here,
these yellow walls of yours are paper thin.
That fantasy picture you loved is just a print.
You owned no originals,
though you talked art.

Your jewellery is costume,
little worth more than fifty euro.
Your clothes, which I thought classy,
are mostly Marks and Spencers.
No designer labels.

This, then, was your life –
one of longings and magpie brightness.
Frugality in a fancy jar.
But the smile, the listening head, the talk, the hands –
these hang in the air indelible,
prismic and precious as diamonds.

BEAUTIFULLY FOR YOU

In a plod, in a plod,
until a high note from the pipes
lifted us into the pure sound of solitude.
Tears fell in veils

as we entered the church behind your coffin.
Inched up the aisle, looking nowhere,
while song came needling the skin
with a baffling, honest pain.

What people said – of nature,
of living finely, of being mindful,
of bursting into infinity
as a creature of light –

couldn't have been more right
if we had cautioned everyone,
on pain of deep regret,
to do it beautifully for you.

They don't come back.
I have yet to see the face of an ancestor
wink and mutter on the wall,
or shimmy through a door like a sword-swipe through cloth.

They won't be peering at you while you sleep,
guiding your working hand
or keeping you from mistakes.
If you have a guardian angel, they're not it.

They're not the bird at your window,
the butterfly on the coffin
or the fly you can't get out of your room.
They are not the newborn child
or the shiver in your spine.

The creature of flesh who walked and spoke –
the now silent creature –
that alone was your beloved.
The most profound mystery
is that she is gone.

SPIRIT

Perhaps you can conceive
that she lives somewhere else in a different form.
Perhaps you're right.
I can't see it,
but there are many things I can't see.

This I can conceive:
that our time together
altered the temper of my brain,
that her movements shifted the air,
helping to press it into a certain shape,
that her voice and touch created waves
and coloured me different.

These corporeal ghosts
have come to live inside me,
bringing her special choice of furniture
and her own, unmistakable scent.

RANT

How dare this person, once of mine,
be silent, adamantine;
the mouth clammed shut, the eyelids closed,
the face hard ice that once was rose!

How dare the world, that promised fun,
deprive me of my precious one,
and set me in a tear of glass,
a dried out remnant of the past!

I'm drawn to your graveside as if you were calling.
I can't bear the thought of you, night after night,
lying there on your own in your new house of oak.
You had wanted to move, have a house in the country.
You've almost achieved it, but at such a price!

You're dying in darkness; the dark's thick outside.
This is hardly your dream of the hollow old tree,
a haven for children, a home for the scared.
Little by little, no matter what effort,
all of our houses will ebb into pulp.

Disappearing Act

Whenever you called, you brought all of you –
your struggles, your joys, your philosophies, your newest reading.
The globe was spun and you beamed out in all directions,
hopping from land to land without warning,
losing the thread, punctuating your travel with laughs.
You listened both well and badly,
remembered details and flavoured them sweet or sour.
The sheer urgent whirlwind did me, your open response,
the way we could leave the house on a ship of talk.

I can't fathom how someone so startlingly there
could suddenly, irrevocably, disappear.

EXTEMPORE

You've torn through the script
of this contemplative production
I call My Life.
I'm pacing like a cat, extemporizing wildly,
wondering what to do now you'll make no entry.

Too melodramatic to tear my hair,
too risqué to tear my clothes,
too uncharacteristic to speak of love,
too close to home to speak of you
and not die.

LEGACY

Your house is shy without you,
a faithful dog with its chin on the ground, waiting.
Your garden is a cat, showing the signs of your care,
licking its copious fur, purring from every pore.

Angela stands at the kitchen window.
On the other side of the glass, the giant lily
graces us with its presence like a pompous courtier,
its trumpet of a mouth turned up.

I see something else:
a new patio, tall potted plants, a herb garden,
a flamboyant, functioning kitchen.
Angela in the centre of it all, her young body singing
its tanned, fruity scent, her face firm and convinced.

What is it parents tell each other?
Hey, you did a good job here.

LOST

Your grave is swaddled in a blanket of flowers.
It's silly to hope they're keeping you warm.
I don't want to leave because, tell the truth,
I'm not coping. I've lost my way.
The map to your grave is the only one I can read.
If my feet don't re-learn to walk,
my only choice will be to lie down here with you.

HOLOGRAM

This moving body they think is me
is only a hologram, well versed in habit.
My real self paces an empty hall,
screaming at the unyielding silence
that shrouds all the most important things.

RAW

Hot water stings, jewellery bites,
towels grate me like cheese.
Sleep is too silent, talk too intense,
walking is shifting tin.

This week I'm so cold I want winter clothes.
What is it you were to me?
A wrap for my shoulders? A moisture cream?
The oil in my bones? My skin?

WHAT HAPPENS

While we look for an agent that moves events,
we must remember this: the world is vast.
At most we have the pieces for one tiny
province of the jigsaw. No-one can know it all.
We admit this when we blame God.
We admit it when we blame a Great Spirit.
We admit it when we blame nothing,
but stare into the fire, wondering what
good was Prometheus' gift
if everyone must die.

This is what I think: fate is how things are.
It's your constitution, your family, your aptitudes.
Everything stems from what has gone before.
The string stretches back to the Big One.
Then, every instant of time is acted upon
by a multitude of forces, only some of which we know.
The sea of the world heaves and ripples;
there's a quick flip, like a woman shaking a blanket,
and your life is altered forever. In another spot,
someone is riding a crest.

Far out in space your feelings are irrelevant.
Fate is what happens. It can't be bad
if it's only a wave in the universal sea.

CAGED SEAS

Smiling came easy to you. You couldn't cry.
You said the tears were stored somewhere inside
in a room long closed.
That caused you pain, as locked rooms do,
all those unshed tears bulging like a caged sea.

I've thought of a smile as a witch's moon
breaking the safe blue of night,
a toboggan ride you can't stop,
a leap into the chasm without a parachute.

Smiling now, I don't know if I'm
burning you into the night-sky
or sending you off the mountain
like a stray stone.

HYPNOTHERAPY

I opened the door of the healing centre and there it was –
your native element, your real home.
Incense rushed through my insides as if it owned me.
African masks, creams, oils, stones and crystals
crowded round, clamouring for attention.
I couldn't sit. I was a stranger.
Bewildered, I wandered the Aladdin's Cave.
So this is what you loved.

The problem was teeth grinding, not you.
The hypnotherapist settled me and we began.
Instantly you were there, in blue and white,
silent and calm at my left side.
You stretched your body and became a planet
where nature's laws were different.
Wolves climbed trees; we could breathe underwater.
You were the sky and the sage that watched.
You would have said you were my guide.

I was befriended by a white wolf, slow and watchful.
We had the same teeth and the same nature,
chewed raw meat and savoured the blood.
When we kissed, our teeth rubbed together
like friendly spears. In his ancient embrace
I told myself he was, at last, the one.
Guide or not, you had led this sceptic
into the shocking realm of peace.

ACCOMPANIED

You grow from the air in fine cafés,
summoned by art; as the forms of the great
rise from the landscape and re-tell it.
You're here at my left side,
head forward, examining things,
wanting to be part, always wanting in.
The music is Chopin, the light Van Gogh,
your empathy a distant, teacher's one,
inclined to help, regardless.

The elements have taken you back,
as though the air had breathed you in.
The café is in Amsterdam.
A gay woman makes eyes at me.
I want to tell you. And also that
these tears are not made of water,
but of light, pattern, space, form
and are beautiful, because
everything natural is everything else.

About the author

Máighréad Medbh was born in Newcastle West, Co. Limerick. Since the publication of her first collection *The Making of a Pagan* (Blackstaff Press, 1990), she has become widely known as a poet who commits a large amount of her creative energy to the performance of her work. She has performed at many venues in Ireland, Great Britain and the United States, and also on broadcast media. Her other collections are *Tenant* (Salmon Poetry, 1999, 2001) and *Split* in the *¡DIVAS! Anthology* (Arlen House, 2003). A CD, *Out of My Skin*, was produced in 2002, and her work is included in a wide range of anthologies. At the moment, Máighréad is also writing for children, and a five part story, set to music, was broadcast by Lyric FM in 2007. In 2008 she received an Annual Bursary from The Arts Council/An Chomhairle Ealaíon. She lives in Swords, County Dublin, and can be contacted at maighreadmedbh@gmail.com.